AN INTRODUCTION TO
DECORATING AND GLAZING POTTERY

A Step-by-Step Guide to Techniques

Caroline Fairbairn

THUNDER BAY
P·R·E·S·S

Published in the United States by
Thunder Bay Press
5880 Oberlin Drive, Suite 400
San Diego, CA 92121-4794
http://www.advmkt.com

ISBN 1-57145-227-3

QUMIDGP

This book was produced by
Quantum Books Ltd
6 Blundell Street
London N7 9BH

Library of Congress Cataloging-in-Publication
Data available upon request.

1 2 3 4 5 99 00 01 02 03

Printed and bound in Singapore by Star Standard Industries Pte Ltd

contents

introduction

Decorating ceramic is a craft as ancient as civilisation itself. From prehistoric times, humans have made and decorated pottery to serve domestic as well as aesthetic needs. Over 80% of our manmade environment consists of ceramic or silica-based materials. Brick, slate and cement can all be classed as a ceramic, so it is understandable therefore that we take it for granted. The purpose of this book is to introduce decorating techniques to help you produce safe, practical pottery and also to encourage you to experiment on your own.

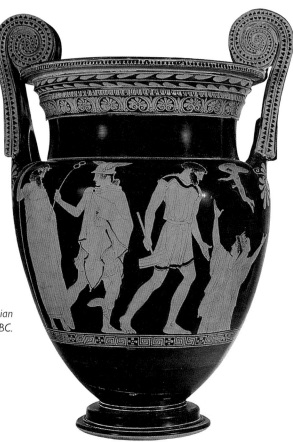

The Creation of Pandora. Athenian vase from the early 5th century BC.

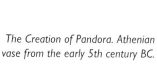

A Brief History of Pottery

ANCIENT

In Ancient societies, notably the Etruscans and Aztecs, the color of the clay formed the basis of the decoration on ceramic, with different clays producing different colors. This color choice, together with patterns scored on the surface of their pots, produced some stunning decoration.

The Greeks and Romans took this a stage further, achieving a larger palette of colors with the introduction of molds. Roman pottery is mainly recognised by its high red gloss appearance.

This was produced by an extremely fine red slip made by settling out fine clay particles in water (terra sigilata).

Tang Dynasty. Earthenware tomb guardian

ORIENTAL

True glazes were first produced in China and the Far East. Early wares used thick, semi-translucent wood ash glazes that picked up the highly modeled surfaces fashionable at the time – a trend that can also be seen in contemporary metal work. Good examples of this are the Celadon wares produced in the 11th to 13th centuries. Only later was the classic blue and white pottery produced.

EUROPEAN

Early European pottery was greatly influenced by Eastern imports, as illustrated by the Delft potters who produced vast quantities of Maiolica to fill the demand for the fashionable oriental style.

The glaze palette of colors increased through experimentation until nearly all colors could be recreated. Europe soon found its own style with great pottery technicians such as Josiah Wedgwood.

MIDDLE EASTERN

Onglaze lustre painting really came into its own in the Islamic world. Here they wanted to recreate metal and glass-work effects on pottery. Ideally situated between the Far East and Europe, potters made use of existing glaze techniques, as well as developing their own. (Safavid, Iznik). Iznik pottery in turn was one of the main influences on the Arts and Crafts potters in Europe.

Contemporary Niger vessel, featuring traditional, symbolic, style and decoration.

Italian inspired, Minton maiolica wine cooler, 1856.

How to use this book

The purpose of this book is to show you how to use glazing and decorating techniques on work that can be either bought, or made yourself. Decorating ceramic can be confusing, as there are many types of clay, methods of firing and glazes that you need to know how to apply. Some people have no interest in making but absolutely love decorating.

The projects are split into three basic sections – Underglaze, Glaze and Onglaze. They are as simple as they sound. Underglaze covers all the decorating methods that can be applied onto unfired clay and unglazed pottery. Glaze means all glazing techniques and methods of glaze decoration. Onglaze means all decorating techniques that are applied to an already glazed surface.

All the projects use an electric kiln, and at the end of the projects section there is a comprehensive section on firing. The projects have been arranged in order of difficulty, beginning with the simplest techniques, and should appeal to the beginner as well as the more seasoned potter. Please pay particular attention to all health and safety advice.

tools and equipment

Setting up the studio

Setting up a work space for decorating ceramic can be both time-consuming and costly if you want to invest in your own kiln, casting and spraying equipment. Most pottery suppliers have a firing and tool hire service, and colleges and schools are sometimes willing to rent firing space as well.

Many tools can be improvised, and where possible cheaper alternatives are suggested. The following text is split into 'decorating tools' and 'basic pottery tools'.

Decorating equipment – banding wheel, slip trailer, masking tape and fluid, brush, toothpicks, sponges, plastic for stencils.

Decorating Tools

SLIP TRAILER	A rubber bladder used for piping slip or glazes onto clay or ceramic.
RUBBER/METAL KIDNEYS	Useful tools when making or decorating. Good for scraping back clay when inlaying or smoothing surfaces, and to force glazes through fine sieves. For a cheap alternative use old phone cards or loyalty cards.
NATURAL SPONGE	Good for many decorating processes. Natural sponges are more effective, as synthetic sponges can leave a residue on the clay when fired.
BRUSHES GENERAL/ FINE ONGLAZE	Try to have separate brushes for the different decorating methods. For fine onglaze decoration try to invest in a good set of soft sable or synthetic brushes.
BRADDLES	These can be bought or you can improvise. Try using old darts or grind the point of an old screwdriver.
BOXWOOD MODELING TOOLS	These tools are made from boxwood because it is very dense and can withstand working on wet material. They are expensive, so a cheaper alternative is to make your own. Old rulers are made from boxwood, and can be cut and sanded to the shape required. With the addition of a metal loop these tools are ideal for hollowing out clay.
METAL MODELING TOOLS	Used for intricate clay and plaster modeling.
STENCILING MATERIAL	You can stencil with most types of paper. For more repetitive stenciling use rubber or heavy duty plastic sacks. This is cheaper than using acetate but you cannot see through the material which can be a disadvantage.

You will need a selection of brush sizes for the various decorating techniques.

BANDING WHEEL/ WHIRLER	It is worth spending a significant amount of money on this tool. It is invaluable for decorating techniques such as banding and all-over lustering. It can also help when decorating items that should be kept free of grease, or items that are too large to move easily.
BUCKETS	A necessity when dipping glazes. Useful for storage and keeping clay damp.
MASKING FLUID	This can be bought from most art shops. The product is latex-based so all brushes should be cleaned in warm soapy water after use.
WAX RESIST	A masking medium especially formulated to burn out in the kiln. This can be bought from pottery suppliers.
MASKING TAPE	Very useful for masking large areas.
100 MESH SIEVE	It is very important to sieve all glazes that you prepare yourself. If you are spraying, no less than a 100 mesh sieve will be suitable. It helps incorporate all the ingredients in the glaze.
MASK/RESPIRATOR	This can be bought from all good hardware stores.

Metal or boxwood modeling tools are used for shaping and etching clay.

Basic Pottery Tools

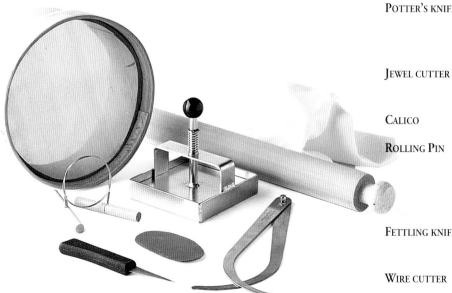

Basic pottery tools - mesh sieve, tile cutter, rolling pin, mask, cheese cutter, potter's knife, rubber kidney, callipers.

POTTER'S KNIFE	Useful for cutting and forming clay objects. It can be bought from pottery suppliers or use an old kitchen knife.
JEWEL CUTTER	Like a pastry cutter, this is used for cutting out shapes in plastic or leather hard clay.
CALICO	Stiff cloth used for rolling out slabs of clay.
ROLLING PIN	Use an old broom handle cut into sections. Wood is the best material for making a rolling pin as it is less likely to stick to the clay surface.
FETTLING KNIFE	A thin-bladed knife used for trimming casts in molds.
WIRE CUTTER	Used for cutting clay and removing wheel thrown pots.
CALLIPERS/METAL RULER	Used for measuring.
WATER SPRAY	Very useful for keeping clay workable when decorating leather hard clay.

decorating materials

(L-R) underglaze color; oxide; onglaze enamel and luster.

All of the following materials can be bought from your local pottery supplier.

Underglaze color

Underglazes are powdered ceramic colors, (also available in tubes in a wet state), that are easy to use under a clear glaze. They are mainly used on plastic, leather or biscuit clay.

Underglazes are extremely suitable for tableware as they will not wear with use. One consideration when using these colors is temperature. Many reds and pinks have a habit of burning out, i.e. the color dilutes or disappears.

Slips

Slips are colored liquid clays used for casting or decorating plastic or leather hard clay. They can be bought commercially or you can make your own. For small amounts an electric hand blender is suitable, but for large amounts of casting slip it is worth investing in a blunger or potter's mixer.

Making decorating slip is quite easy. Simply wet down clay with water to the required consistency. To make different colors you can add oxides or body stains. The consistency for decorating depends on the job the slip is going to do.

Try experimenting with glazes to find the color you prefer.

DECORATING METHOD	CONSISTENCY
Color washes	milk
Painting	light cream
Slip-trailing	heavy cream
Casting	light cream

The actual underglaze color may differ slightly in tone from the packet.

Body stains

Body stains are similar to underglaze colors and are bought in powder form. They are mixed into clay, glazes or slips to produce a range of colors. Try adding 4-10% in a glaze (dry weight to dry weight), and 5-15% in clay bodies and slips. The color intensity depends on the amount of body stain added, so testing is always advisable. You can always add more color to the mix but you cannot remove it. It is a good idea to sieve the mix when using stains in glazes and slips to encourage an even dispersal of the color.

Adding color to clay is slightly more complex. Divide a manageable amount of clay in half using a wire cutter. Sprinkle the surface with some of the body stain to be added and put the two halves together. Repeat until all of the stain has been incorporated into the clay. Wedge (knead) the clay together until no streaks of color are left. You can repeat this process until you have reached the color intensity required.

Glazes come in a variety of colors.

Oxides

Oxides are elements combined with oxygen that give us the main coloring agents used in ceramics. All underglazes, stains, colored glazes, enamels and lusters have oxide components in them.

The following chart indicates the usual colors produced by oxides.

OXIDE	NOTES	COLOR	GUIDE ON % USED
Antimony	...	Naples yellow	10-20%
Cadmium	Very poisonous	Vivid red	*
Cobalt	Acts as a flux	Blue/black	1-3%
Chromium	...	Greens/pink when added to tin glaze	1-3%
Copper	Dangerous when added to tin glaze	...	1-5%
Iron	...	Red/yellow/black	2-10%
Manganese	...	Coffee	$1/_4$ - 5%
Nickel	Carcinogenic raw	Blue/pink/rusty pink	1-3%
Uranium	Radioactive	Red/orange	*
Vanadium	...	Yellow	10%

Not usually available but are included in commercially produced glazes

The base glaze that oxides are added to can drastically affect the outcome of the color produced. For example, chrome, which usually produces a vivid green color, will turn pink when added to a tin glaze. (Please refer to Health and Safety section, 'Metal Release').

Glazes

A glaze is basically a glass that is applied to a biscuited clay surface. It makes clay surfaces impervious to water. Glazes can be bought in powder form or ready-mixed with a water medium for immediate use. There are thousands of types of glaze producing many colors and textures. Glazes are basically grouped into two categories – 'stoneware' and 'earthenware'. Earthenware glazes are fired in a low temperature range and stoneware in a higher. Within these ranges there are even more sub-groups giving various textures and effects.

Luster

Lusters are a mixture of resin and soluble salts that, once fired, leave a metallic residue on the surface of the glaze. They come in many solid metallic forms like gold or an iridescent mother-of-pearl effect. Modern commercial lusters can be fired in an electric kiln. These have taken the difficulty out of applying lusters on glazed ceramic. Earlier methods were very hit and miss affairs, with low success rates requiring a gas kiln.

A wide range of lusters is also readily available.

Luster effects can be stunning.
Paul J. Katrich. Lustred Bowl.

Enamels

Enamels are colors with a high glass content which are applied to a glazed surface. Oil or water-based, enamels can be bought in powder or tube form. There is little variation once fired from initial application. Ensure that the glazed surfaces you are decorating are grease and dust free. You will often find that some colors do not mix with each other. Usually oranges and reds cannot be mixed with blues and earth colors. This is often because the colors are cadmium/selenium based. Please ensure all the enamels you use on tableware are suitable. (See Health and Safety section, ('Metal Release'). As with lusters, it is advisable to have separate brushes for application.

ready to decorate

You can decorate clay in two states 'raw' and 'fired'. The following describes these states.

Underglaze

PLASTIC CLAY

Plastic is the term we use for moldable wet clay. When visiting your pottery supplier you will see clays labeled according to their use or color. All clays will have their maturing firing temperature clearly labeled. If you are in any doubt, do not hesitate to ask the supplier which clay is more suitable for the type of making you are doing.

Plastic clay is used for throwing pots on the potter's wheel and modeling. It is the first stage of all ceramic making. When building anything out of plastic clay, it is important that its consistency is correct. It must be smooth and contain no air bubbles. One way to ensure this is to wedge, or knead the clay to improve its consistency. In some ceramic books this is likened to kneading bread. However the objective is the complete opposite. The aim is to remove trapped air not incorporate it.

Mouldable wet or 'plastic' clay is available in different colors.

LEATHER HARD

When potters refer to clay as 'leather hard', they are describing its consistency. This state is when the clay has dried a little, leaving it stiff but still workable. 'Cheesy' is another way of describing leather hard clay. This state is ideally suited for building techniques such as slabbing, turning footrings on hand thrown pots, and certain methods of decoration. One quick way of producing leather hard clay objects is by casting them in molds. When drying complicated shapes to a leather hard state, try and do this slowly as a variable thickness will cause your work to crack. This is especially true on items that have handles. Dry the work in a 'damp cupboard', or under plastic.

The slab on the right shows how your leather hard clay should look. The slab on the left is too dry.

Glaze

BISCUIT

'Biscuit' is the term potters use when describing clay that has been fired once, to a mid-temperature of around 1000ºC. This is the state of ceramic when glazes and under glazes are usually applied. It is called 'biscuit' because of its porous quality and, just like when you dunk a donut into a cup of coffee, biscuit ceramic will suck a glaze onto its surface. It is important that you do not exceed 1000ºC in this initial firing as it will cause the surface to vitrify. Vitrification is where the clay starts to turn into a glass. Glazes will not stick if you try to apply them to a pot fired higher than 1000ºC.

You can make your own ceramic objects and then biscuit fire them, or you can buy ready made blanks. These can be purchased from your local pottery supplier, or there are now many 'paint your own' tableware companies.

GLAZED BLANKS

A glazed blank is anything you make or buy that has a smooth glazed surface suitable for onglaze decoration. This means you can buy an entire dinner service and personalise it with enamels or lusters. It also means that you can buy and decorate more complicated ceramic objects, such as lamp bases. Make sure you remove any electrical hardware before decorating. They do not have to be white but the background will affect the decorating material color if it is not opaque.

Decorating processes suitable for glazed blanks are:

- Enamel pointillism – applying dots of enamel
- free hand enamel and luster painting
- Banding enamels and lusters

Any size or type of glazed blank can be bought or made.

Banding is a simple, yet effective technique.

health and safety

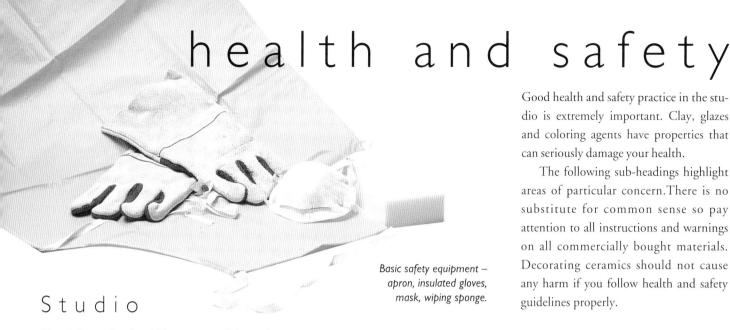

Good health and safety practice in the studio is extremely important. Clay, glazes and coloring agents have properties that can seriously damage your health.

The following sub-headings highlight areas of particular concern. There is no substitute for common sense so pay attention to all instructions and warnings on all commercially bought materials. Decorating ceramics should not cause any harm if you follow health and safety guidelines properly.

Basic safety equipment – apron, insulated gloves, mask, wiping sponge.

Studio

- The studio should be warm, well-lit and well-ventilated.
- Much of the equipment and raw materials are heavy, so take care when moving or lifting.
- The most important tools you use are your hands. Decorating or making ceramic requires you to work in damp conditions. Clay can suck the moisture and oils from your hands, which can cause your skin to crack or become sore. Wear gloves when possible, or protect your hands with barrier cream especially designed for wet work.
- Using a 'dolly' or porter's trolley can prevent backache when lifting heavy materials.

Corrosive

Silica

One of the most important health and safety considerations is silica, as it can be breathed in, causing silicosis, a lung disease that also affects miners. Silica is the main constituent of clay and can also be found in glazes, ceramic fiber, quartz, flint, feldspar and asbestos.

Precautions
- Dry clay should never be worked.
- Dusty surfaces should be cleaned with a damp sponge or mop.
- Good quality respirators or masks should be worn when cleaning floors or spraying any silica-based material.

Lead

Many glazes contain lead, and although it is a very useful ceramic material, it can cause poisoning if ingested. Raw lead can now be safely substituted with fritted compounds that are relatively safe to use. A frit is essentially a glass. Raw materials are melted together, then shattered, and ground to fine powder. This makes the lead component less ingestible but still should be treated with caution. (See 'Metal Release').

Toxic

Precautions
- Always wear a mask when spraying glazes to avoid breathing in the lead.
- Never eat, drink, or smoke in the studio.
- Check the suitability of the glaze for tableware.
- When in doubt, most pottery suppliers have glaze testing facilities for tableware.
- Use safer methods of glazing such as dipping or brushing.

Metal Release

Poisonous metal can leach out when in contact with acid foodstuffs. This is known as metal release. Therefore not all glazes are suitable for tableware.

Precautions

- Always check suitability of a glaze when applying to tableware.
- Do not add copper to a lead glaze, as this increases the release factor, and makes it highly poisonous.
- Red and yellow colors require special attention as they often contain cadmium which is extremely poisonous and not suitable for tableware.

Fire

Fumes and Ventilation

It is important when firing and decorating ceramics that you are in a well-ventilated environment. Reduction firing can produce carbon monoxide which can kill if over-exposed. Commercially bought lusters are in a medium that can cause irritation to the nose and eyes. Also, when these are fired they can produce chlorine and sulphur fumes.

Precautions

- Always well-ventilate the studio when firing.
- When decorating with noxious mediums, e.g. acetone, the best place is outside in an open environment.
- The use of extractor fans can aid in the ventilation of the studio.

Goggles make checking your kiln easier, as well as safer.

ALWAYS READ THE SAFETY WARNING LABELS ON YOUR EQUIPMENT AND MATERIALS.

underglaze

Introduction

The term 'underglaze' simply describes all methods of decoration that can be applied under a glaze. You can mold, color, scribe and mark unfired clay in many different decorative ways.

This book concentrates on methods of surface decoration, and to do this you first need clay objects on which to work. A quick way is by using molds. Molds are useful ways of making tableware that can then be decorated. These can be bought or you can make your own. Consistent results can be achieved by pressing in clay or casting slip.

*Janet Hamer.
Drake Mandarin with
Sunflowers. Slip-painted
with wax-resist glazes.*

Making your own molds

A mold is the negative of the shape you want to make. Before you can make a mold you need to make the shape first, or find a suitable object that will perform the same function. We call these 'shape former' models. For molding it is better to make your model out of clay, as it is easy to remove. To make your own molds you will need some plaster of Paris, water, shoring boards or vinyl and some spare clay.

Frank Hamer. Plate with three speckled soap-fish. Colored slips under a transparent glaze.

1 Make a bowl shape out of a solid piece of clay, or use a ready-made pottery blank.

2 Place this rim down on a board or covered table. A coating of shilac or pva can be applied to seal the board and aid release.

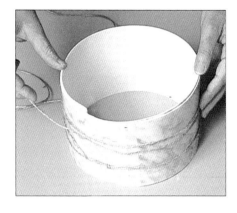

3 Shore up the model with vinyl leaving a two inch gap around the side. To support the boards you can use bricks or tie them together so they hold their shape firmly.

4 Now you must ensure that there are no gaps for the plaster of Paris to escape through. Seal all seams with clay where the vinyl comes into contact with the table surface.

5 Now mix up the plaster. Wear a good mask as you do not want the plaster dust to get into your lungs. Try and guesstimate how many pints of plaster you will need by eye. Tapping the bucket will release any trapped air bubbles in the mixture. Remember the warmer the water and the faster you stir, the quicker the plaster will set (go off). When the plaster starts to thicken you can pour it over the model.

6 When the plaster is set, remove the model.

You will now have a negative of the clay bowl. It will only be ready to use when it has thoroughly dried two or three days in a warm place. You can press clay or cast into the mold using slip.

How to make casting slip

You can buy casting slip or you can make your own.

A defloccuant is added to a wet clay mixture to keep the clay particles in suspension and aid fluidity. Too much defloccuant and the mix gets too viscous. Too little defloccuant and the clay settles out of suspension. The ratio of water, clay and defloccuant therefore is very important. This is a useful formulae but when in doubt buy readily prepared slip.

Frank Hamer. Plate with two Bitterling. Colored slips under a transparent glaze.

WEIGHT OF CLAY	AMOUNT OF WATER	SODIUM SILICATE @ 140TW*	SODA ASH@140TW*
13lb	½ pint	0.2 oz	0.2 oz
26lb	1 pint	0.4 oz	0.2 oz
52lb	2 pints	1 oz	0.8 oz

*TW is the annotation for Twaddell, a unit used to measure suspensions and solutions.

Once you have finished making your casting or decorating slip it is important that you sieve the mixture before use. This ensures equipment does not clog and you have consistent decorating and making results.

Janet Hamer. Cruising Carolina.
Slip and glaze.

impressive leaves

This is a gentle introduction to decorating pottery. Choose leaves with pronounced veins, as they will look more effective. You can use all kinds of textured surfaces for decorating plastic clay. Shells, bark or even lace will create a stunning pattern on your pottery.

underglaze

you will need

- [ ] White plastic clay
- [ ] Rolling out cloth
- [ ] Rolling pin
- [ ] Tile cutter
- [ ] Selection of leaves
- [ ] Copper carbonate
- [ ] Clear glaze
- [ ] Fine brush

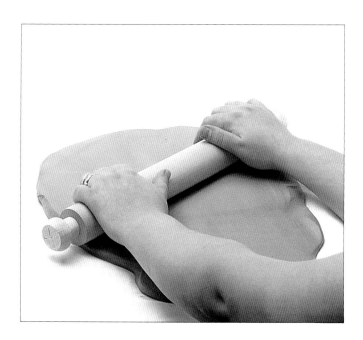

1. First roll out a slab of clay, to a thickness of about one finger. Do this on a cloth to prevent the clay from sticking to the surface.

2. To make sure the slab is big enough, size it up by using the tile cutter. You will need enough clay to make four tiles Make sure clay thickness is even..

3   Now lay a selection of leaves on the clay, with the prominent veins facing downwards.

4   Using the rolling pin, gently roll the leaves into the clay. Make sure that the leaves are well-spaced.

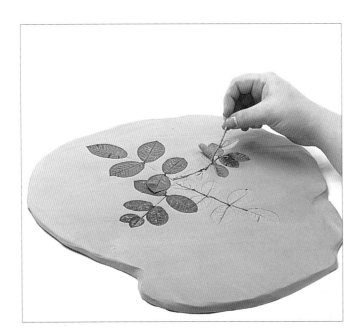

5   Remove the leaves by gently teasing them out by their stalks. It is important not to mark the surface of the clay, or smudge the delicate impression. Now cut out the panel using the tile cutter.

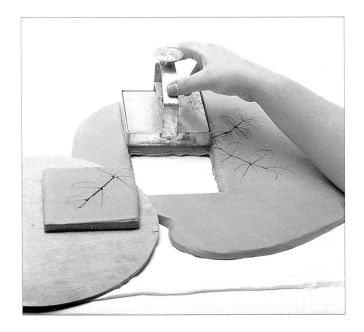

6   Once the tiles have air dried to leather hard consistency, add a wash of oxide over the leaf impression. Mix $1/_5$ oz (5g) of copper carbonate with 3 fl oz (100 ml) of water. Gently paint this onto the leaf shapes. Because the solution is so weak the oxide will settle into the veins of the leaves highlighting them.

7 Now allow the tiles to dry completely so they are ready to biscuit fire. Once they have been fired they should be clear glazed. Hold the tile firmly by the edges and dip into the clear glaze. Make sure that you clean any excess glaze off the bottom before firing.

When finished, tiles can be mounted or framed. Individual tiles can also be decorated

sponge printed beaker

Printing is one of the most effective ways of producing uniform decoration on ceramic. It is therefore especially suited to tableware when you need to make several matching pieces. Simple, bold shapes work best with this technique.

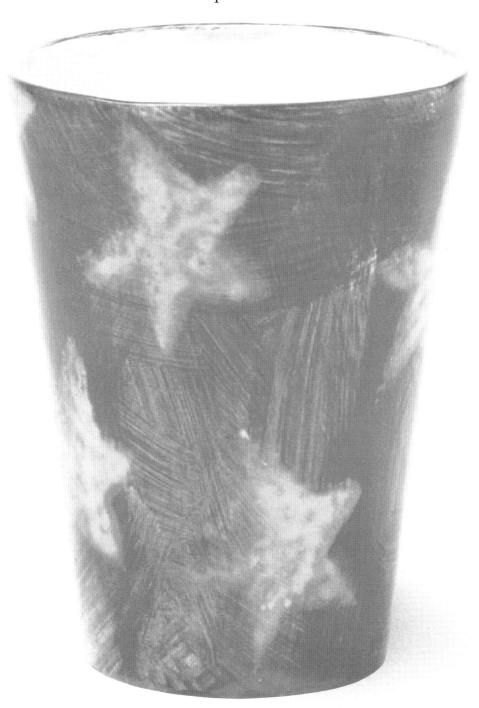

underglaze

you will need

- ☐ Marker pen
- ☐ Sponge
- ☐ Leather hard beaker
- ☐ Blue and yellow underglazes
- ☐ Scalpel or craft knife
- ☐ Wide brush
- ☐ Paper towels
- ☐ Clear glaze

1 First make the shape that you are going to print with. To do this, clearly mark out your shape in pen on a scouring sponge.

2 Then carefully cut out the design using a craft knife or scalpel. It is useful to have spare sponge pieces in case of mistakes.

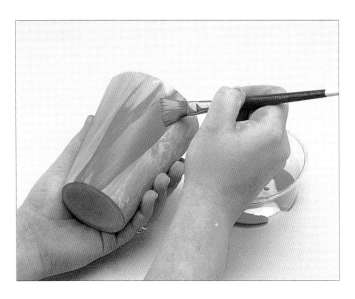

3 Brush an all-over wash of the blue underglaze onto the outside of the beaker. Keep your brush strokes as even as possible. Do not overload your brush.

4 Use the shape to print a random pattern all over the beaker. Allow to dry and then biscuit fire. Clear glaze the beaker and refire.

slip trailed panel

This project shows the method of slip-trailing. It is a versatile technique that can be used to great effect when writing text or outlining a design on ceramic. You can use this process on upright objects, as well as on panels.

you will need

- ☐ Terracotta clay
- ☐ Rolling pin
- ☐ Rolling-out cloth
- ☐ Sieve
- ☐ Slip trailer
- ☐ Potter's knife
- ☐ Slip
- ☐ Scribe
- ☐ Clear glaze

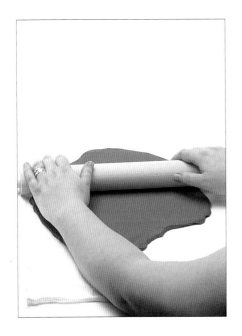

1 First roll out a slab of clay to about finger thickness. Ensure that the thickness is even all over the rolled-out slab.

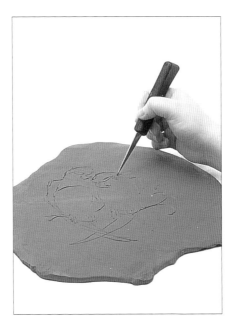

2 Now mark out your design onto the slab. Use a scribe to do this. This scores the surface to act as a key when applying the slip. See template page 127.

3 Fill the slip trailer with thickly sieved slip. Test this slip on a scrap piece of clay before applying to your slab. This allows you to practise the technique.

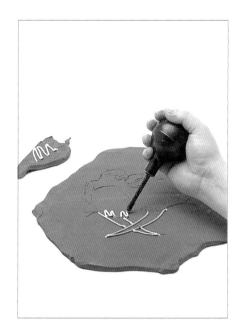  

4   Pipe over the marks on the slab of clay. An even pressure on the slip trailing bladder ensures even results.

5   Once you have finished piping the design onto the slab you must let it dry to a leather hard consistency.

6   Once it has dried, cut out the shape required with the potter's knife. Allow to dry completely, then biscuit fire. Clear glaze, and fire.

stenciling a bowl

When using a paper stencil, it is important that the clay is not too dry, or the paper will not stick. Keep your paper shapes simple for the most effective use of this technique.

underglaze

you will need

- ☐ Leather hard clay bowl
- ☐ Two contrasting underglaze colors lime green, turquoise
- ☐ Paper
- ☐ Scalpel
- ☐ Water
- ☐ Sponge
- ☐ Clear glaze

1 Mark out paper shapes to your chosen design. Using a scalpel and ruler, cut out these shapes out carefully.

2 Sponge a color all over the leather hard bowl and allow to dry for a couple of minutes. Ensure that you have sponged an even coating.

3 Dip the paper shapes into water and squeeze off excess. If they are too wet, the next glaze coat will not dry evenly.

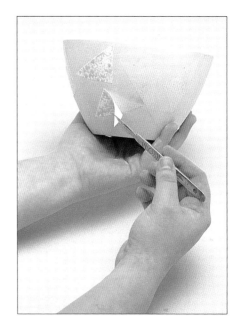

4   Then apply these paper shapes to the bowl surface. The paper should stick to the surface of the bowl. Make sure the shapes are smooth and not wrinkled.

5   Now sponge a contrasting underglaze color all over the bowl. Ensure this coat completely covers the paper shapes.

6   Remove the paper shapes gently using a scalpel. Be careful not to scratch the bowl surface. Now dry in preparation for biscuit firing.

relief model sun

This project shows you the technique of sticking clay to clay. It can be used both to decorate, and to add structures such as handles on mugs, or spouts on pots. It is a vital technique to master, as work that seems fine before firing will separate and split if joins are not made correctly.

you will need

- ☐ Rolling pin
- ☐ Rolling out cloth
- ☐ Scribe/toothpick
- ☐ Potter's knife
- ☐ Slip
- ☐ Modeling tools

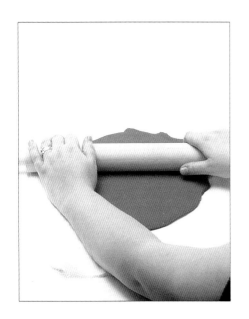

1 First roll out a slab of clay to finger thickness, ensuring that thickness is consistent throughout the slab.

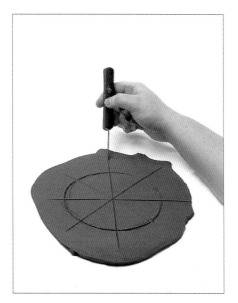

2 Using the scribe, draw a circle onto the clay and divide this first into half, then into quarters and then into eighths. This is only a guide, so a rough drawing will do.

3 Now mark eight triangles on the outside edge of the circle. Use a toothpick to etch fine lines.

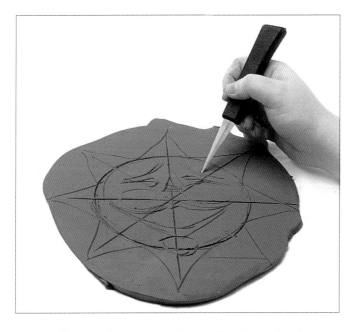

4 Draw in the features of a laughing face using the potter's knife. If you make a mistake, simply smooth over with your finger and start again. See template shown on p128.

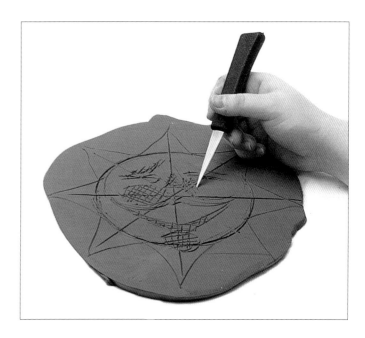

5 Relief modeling is where we add clay to a flat surface. To help this clay stick to the surface, score the surface with the potter's knife. Every highlighted area of the face which will have clay added in relief will need surface scoring.

6 Also apply a runny slip to the scored areas, to help adhesion.

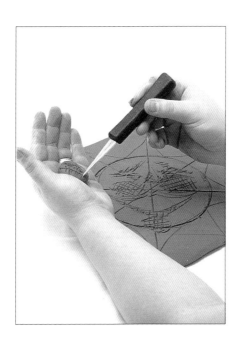

7 Make sure the clay pieces you are going to add have also been scored. This will ensure adhesion is secure.

8 Using the slip, add clay to the areas that you have scored.

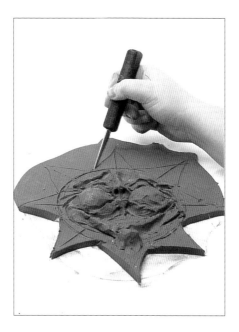

9 Once enough clay has been added you can model the features 'free-hand'. Mold them using the modeling tools, or even your fingers.

10 Once you are happy with your modeled features, use the potter's knife to cut out the sun.

11 Leave your sun to slowly dry. Once dry it is read for biscuit firing and clear glazing.

A relief moon complements this project perfectly. See template on p129.

banded plate

This project will familiarise you with the banding wheel as an invaluable decorating tool. A heavy banding wheel will work best with this project as it will have a greater momentum, meaning it will keep turning for longer.

you will need

- ☐ Leather hard plate
- ☐ Two complementary underglaze colors leaf green, lime green
- ☐ Water spray
- ☐ Wide brush
- ☐ Banding wheel
- ☐ Clear glaze

1 Center the leather hard plate on the banding wheel. If the plate is not properly centered it will not rotate evenly, and may even slide off the wheel.

2 Lightly spray the plate with water. This will ensure that the color you are going to apply will glide freely.

3   Spin the banding wheel and apply one color with the brush, starting from the center. Spin the wheel steadily to ensure an even color distribution.

4   Gently move your hand from the center to the outside edge, stopping about half way. Clean the brush before applying the second color.

5   Now load the brush with the second underglaze color. Spin the banding wheel again and apply the color, moving the brush this time towards the center of the plate.

6   Stop the wheel when the two colors meet. Let the plate dry ready for firing, then clear glaze.

When you are happy with this technique, you can experiment with different color combinations.

sgraffito bowl

This project utilises one of the most popular forms of decoration. Sgrafitto means 'to scratch' and the method is as simple as it sounds. You can scratch through slips or underglazes. Make sure you use a base color that contrasts with the color of your clay.

you will need

- ☐ Leather hard bowl
- ☐ Banding wheel
- ☐ Scribe
- ☐ Red and brown underglaze colors
- ☐ Wide brush
- ☐ Fine brush
- ☐ Clear glaze (if required)

1   Place your leather hard bowl at the center of the banding wheel, rim downwards. Band two panels of red underglaze onto the bowl.

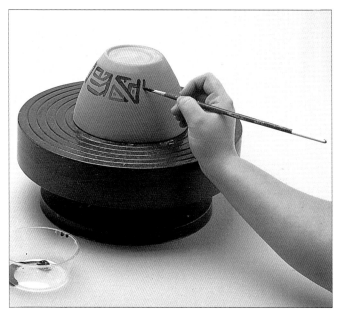

2   Paint 'free-hand' geometric patterns onto these banded panels using the brown underglaze. See template shown on p136.

3   When you have completed these patterns, allow them to dry for a couple of minutes.

4   Then, using a scalpel or potter's knife, score around the patterns through to the clay underneath.

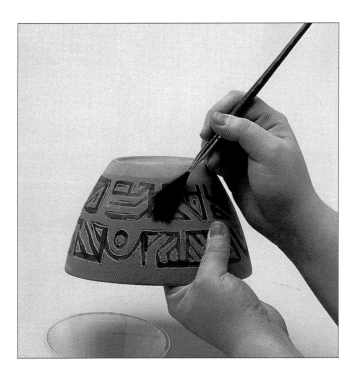

5   Remove the residue using a soft brush. Do not attempt to blow residue away, as this could spoil your pattern. Slowly dry and biscuit fire.

This sgraffito technique can be used on any object. You can clear glaze if you wish, but an unglazed finish gives vessels a more 'ethnic' look.

combed platter

Combing is a traditional English form of decoration, popularised in the 17th Century on Staffordshire earthenware. Because of the speed required for this form of decoration, it is advisable to first practise on some scrap clay.

you will need

- [ ] Soft leather hard plate
- [ ] Two colored runny slips white and blue
- [ ] Jug
- [ ] Soft brush
- [ ] Plastic bowl

1 This is a very instantaneous form of decoration so it is important that you have all the materials at hand.

2 First you will need to pour the slip all over the plate surface. Allow the excess to run off into the plastic bowl.

3 Now, dribble the colored slip randomly over the surface of the plate.

4 Using a soft brush, manipulate the wet surface of the clay, slightly mixing the two colors together.

5 The plate will need to be dried slowly as this technique has a habit of cracking if rushed. Do this by placing the plate in a plastic bag and leave to dry for a couple of weeks. It is now ready to fire and clear glaze.

The combing techniques can be as colorful as you wish!

wax resist

Building up color and design can be achieved with great
effect using wax resist emulsion. For this technique you
need to be able to think in reverse, as the last color you
apply will appear as the background color.

you will need

- [ ] Leather hard vase
- [ ] Wax resist
- [ ] Underglaze colors
  brown, orange, yellow
- [ ] Medium brush
- [ ] Fine brush
- [ ] Sponges
- [ ] Clear glaze

1 Using the medium brush, wash over the whole of the vase with an underglaze color. Apply this coat evenly, and do not overload your brush.

2 Using the fine brush, paint random spirals of wax resist over the surface of the vase. Allow the wax resist to dry before continuing. This should only take a couple of minutes.

3   Now sponge a second color over the entire vase. Again, make sure you apply the coat evenly.

4   Repeat the process of applying wax resist in spirals. Keep your pattern simple as this will give a more pleasing effect.

5   Now sponge the brown underglaze over the whole of the vessel. This is the last layer of color to be added.

tartan ware

As with tartan cloth, different colored underglazes can be overlaid to give the impression of a weave. Try using semi-transparent underglazes in this project – they work well with this technique.

underglaze

you will need

- ☐ Leather hard mug
- ☐ Dark green underglaze
- ☐ Light green underglaze
- ☐ Wide brush
- ☐ Lining brush
- ☐ Banding wheel
- ☐ Clear glaze

1   With the help of the banding wheel, paint a horizontal line on the mug with the dark green underglaze. Start and finish at the handle.

2   Repeat this down the mug, leaving a small gap between each line. Try to keep these lines as evenly spaced as possible.

3 Now paint vertical stripes around the mug, again start-ing at the handle. Leave a gap between the lines.

4 Change to the light green underglaze and repeat the previous steps, painting in the gaps between the dark green lines first horizontally.

5 Then paint in the vertical lines as shown in step 3.

6 Once the mug has dried for a couple of minutes, use the lining brush to paint horizontal blue lines.

7 Paint vertical blue lines to create a chequer effect. The mug is now ready to be dried, biscuit fired and clear glazed.

intaglio pot

This project introduces you to the carving techniques of leather hard clay. Carved ceramic really shows up semi-transparent and stoneware glazes that vary in color with thickness. For really crisp carving, the clay should be in a 'hard' leather hard state.

underglaze

you will need

- ☐ Leather hard lidded pot or box
- ☐ Linoleum cutting tools
- ☐ Scribe
- ☐ Transparent colored glaze

1   Using the scribe, draw three circles on the pot. These circles should be quite small. Place them anywhere you choose.

2   You will be decorating the whole pot, so the circles can overlap the body of the pot and the lid. Use the template shown on p130 if you wish

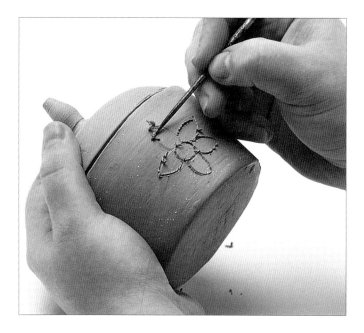

3   Draw small petals around each of these circles. The petals should be the same size and be evenly spaced.

4   Now draw in larger petals around the smaller petals. You can spread these up and over the lid.

5   Draw a pattern of swirls between the flowers. Make sure your etched lines do not overlap if possible.

6   Now the design has been marked out, use the linoleum tools to carve out the flower design. You will need to carve quite deeply for the best effect.

7   The pot is now ready to dry, biscuit fire and glaze. Try and use a transparent colored glaze as this will pick up the surface detail well.

combined techniques

This project shows you how to mix several techniques to great effect on a single piece of ceramic. You have now hopefully developed a wide repertoire of techniques, and found those which suit you best.

underglaze

you will need

- [ ] Banding wheel
- [ ] Leather hard plate
- [ ] Underglaze colors
  – blue, sea green, turquoise
- [ ] Plastic for stencil
- [ ] Marker pen
- [ ] Craft knife
- [ ] Lining brush
- [ ] Permanent marker
- [ ] Sponge
- [ ] Clear glaze

1   Put the leather hard plate on to the banding wheel, and band blue all over the plate (see 'Banding a plate' for instructions).

2   Using the lining brush and the turquoise underglaze, paint wavy horizontal lines all over the plate.

3   Cut out a round piece of plastic, the same size as the plate. On one half of this plastic draw the outline of a fish. See template shown on p131.

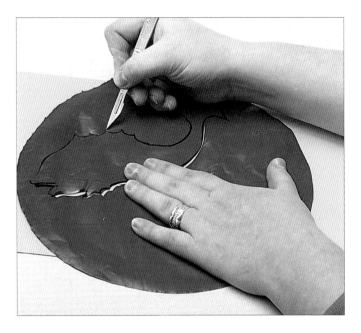

4   Cut out the fish using a craft knife. Hold the plastic steady and cut gently but firmly.

5   The hole remaining will act as your stencil. Make sure you have spare plastic available to practise on if you wish.

6   Place the stencil on the plate, and sponge over using the turquoise underglaze color.

7   Allow to dry for a couple of minutes. This will prevent the pattern smearing when you apply the next stencil.

8   Then turn the stencil 180° and repeat previous step.

9   You will now have two fish on your plate. Allow paint to dry.

10   Being carefully not to overload with paint, use the lining brush to outline each fish.

11   Paint in the scales and fins and allow to dry ready for biscuit firing and clear glazing.

glaze

Silsal Ceramics, Jordan. Hand built stoneware vases with a smooth matte glaze.

Introduction

Glazes are put onto ceramic to color, or protect the surface, allowing it to be used for many different functions. The first glazes were probably happy accidents of the firing process. Wood burnt in the kiln was found to react with the surface of the clay producing a natural glass-forming combination. Today the range of glazes is phenomenal – every conceivable color and texture can bought.

Some glazes are more suitable for certain jobs than others. It is important to bear this in mind when you are decorating your work. Stoneware glazes are very useful on ceramic that has to withstand massive temperature changes. This is because it is fired to such a high temperature that the clay itself vitrifies (turns to stone) so moisture cannot permeate into the ceramic itself. This reduces the effect of frost damage at one extreme, and allows you to make oven proof dishes at the other. Earthenware glazes are good for tableware and are more cost effective than higher temperature glazes as the fuel for the firing will be less.

Using a glaze

Brushing on a glaze is probably the easiest method for the beginner. Apply some common sense, and use a large brush when covering large areas. Methodically paint 2-3 even coats, allowing time to dry between each coat.

Sieve glazes when you have mixed them up yourself in a fine sieve.

Dipping is probably the most efficient form of all-over glazing. The consistency of the glaze should be very thin, like milk. Try and hold the work firmly with one hand and dip into the glaze for a couple of seconds. When you remove the piece of work from the glaze allow the shine to fade. It is now safe to handle without marking the surface of the glaze. Touch up the areas where you held the pot with glaze using a brush or finger. For larger pieces of work pour the glaze onto your piece using a jug, rotating at the same time over a container. Repeat this process on the inside and the outside. Make sure you clean off the glaze from the bottom of your pots before firing.

Spraying is a process not recommended for the beginner. You will need a compressor, spray gun and spray booth. Air brushing effects can be achieved by sponging and stenciling. If you do have access to the specialist equipment required, when spraying try to move in smooth positive strokes 10-12 inches away from the ceramic. Flush the spray gun through with clean water when finished.

Most glazes should only be the thickness of cartridge paper. One way of testing this is to scratch the surface with a pin. Now you can see how thick the glaze is, remove the mark by rubbing with a finger.

Caroline Fairbairn. Glazed terracotta pots.

Mark Smith. Salt glazed bowl. This is an advanced technique requiring a gas kiln.

Mark Smith. Salt glazed vessel.

Problems with glazes

CRAWLING

This is where areas of the glaze crawl back once fired, exposing the clay body. Causes of this can be that the glaze has been too thickly applied, or that the surface of the biscuit ceramic was greasy.

ORANGE PEEL

This is where the surface of a smooth glaze appears dimpled. This is caused by the glaze being too thickly applied.

MATTE GLOSS GLAZE

This can be caused by the kiln not reaching the maturing temperature of the glaze.

Silsal Ceramics. Stoneware salad bowls inspired by bronze age pottery. Incised with matte glaze.

COLOR OF THE GLAZE IS WEAK OR HAS DISAPPEARED

This can be caused by the glaze being too thin when it was applied. Some colors, for example reds, have a habit of burning out (disappearing) when they have been over-fired.

two tone bowl

This project introduces you to the idea of overlaying one glaze onto another. It is vital that you test glaze combinations before applying them to tableware (see Health and Safety chapter). All glazes that are to be dipped should be sieved before use.

you will need

- ☐ Biscuit fired bowl
- ☐ Two same-temperature glazes (blue and green).
- ☐ Two containers
- ☐ Wax resist

1   Mix up the glazes (see Health and Safety - 'glazes') into containers big enough to take the size of bowl you are going to decorate. They should have the consistency of milk with no lumps. Sieving will help this.

2   Now paint the foot ring using the wax resist emulsion. This will prevent the bowl sticking to the kiln shelf, as it will keep glaze off the footring.

3   Hold the bowl by placing your thumb on the rim and your fingers on the foot ring. Now dip approximately half the bowl into the glaze.

4   Leave it submerged for a few seconds and then remove. Allow to drain.

5   When the shine has faded from the glaze it is safe to handle. Rotate bowl 180° and repeat dipping process with the second glaze. Ensure that glazes overlap.

6   Allow to drain. When drained completely, set aside to dry.

7   When the shine has faded from this glaze it is ready to glaze fire.

mosaic flower pot

Dividing the surface of a vessel can be very difficult. This project shows how to divide a pot into small even sections. This process can also be used on flat surfaces such as plates. The glazes you use must be opaque to contrast well with the dark terracotta background.

you will need

- ☐ Terracotta flower pot
- ☐ Paper
- ☐ Marker pen
- ☐ Ruler
- ☐ Two opaque glazes blue, green
- ☐ Sponge
- ☐ Scalpel

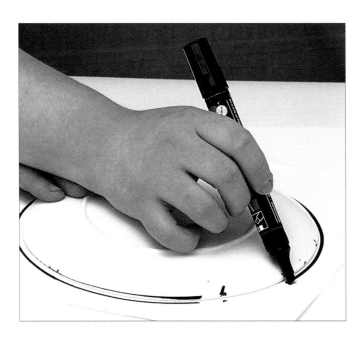

1   Draw around a dinner plate to draw a circle wider than the rim of your flower pot.

2   Using a ruler and pencil, divide this circle into half, then into quarters, into eighths and finally into sixteenths.

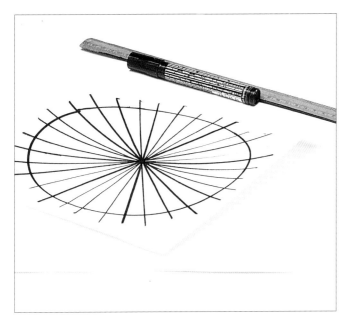

3 The result should look like the spokes on a wheel. This is your guide for the decoration.

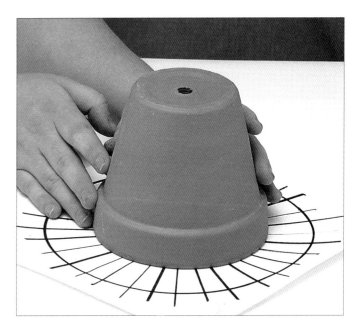

4 Place the flower pot upside down on the paper grid. Make sure the pot is centerd on the guide.

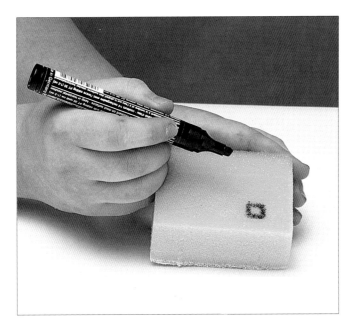

5 Now mark out your square stamp on the sponge using the marker pen. This should be a little smaller than the sections on your guide. For instructions on making this stamp, see Underglaze Project 2.

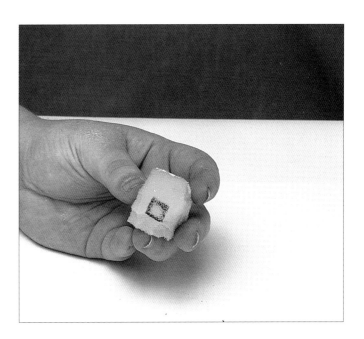

6 Carefully cut out the sponge stamp using your scalpel. Leave enough sponge to let you hold the stamp comfortably.

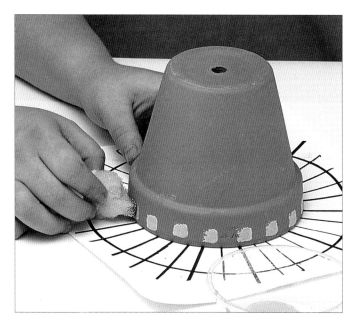

7 Starting at the top of the flower pot, use the guide to print squares of the first colored glaze in every other section.

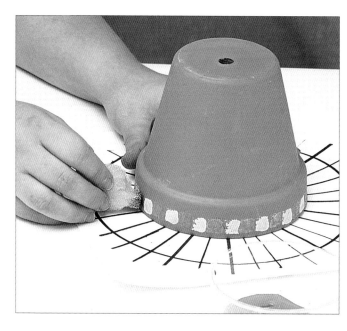

8 Now print squares of the second color glaze between the squares of the first color.

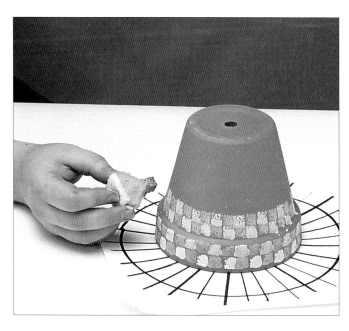

9 Once you have the first line of squares, repeat the decoration down the flower pot, alternating the colors. This will build up the mosaic pattern. The pot is now ready for glaze firing.

patterned flower pot

When choosing a flower pot to decorate, it is important to check for any cracks in the clay. One way to find out is by holding the pot lightly at the base and flicking the rim. If it rings with a clear note there are no cracks. If the sound is dull, choose another pot.

you will need

- ☐ Terracotta flower pot
- ☐ Sponge
- ☐ brush
- ☐ An opaque glaze
- ☐ Masking tape - two sizes

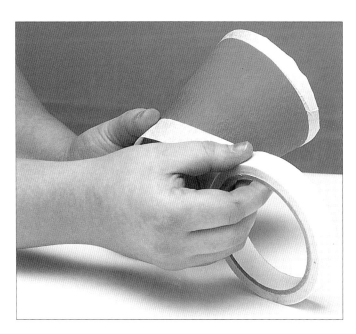

1   Mask the rim and foot of the pot with the thicker tape. Make sure tape is placed evenly.

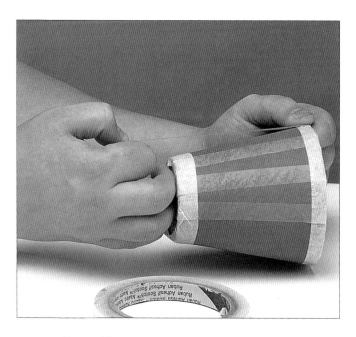

2   Now stick vertical strips of fine tape down the side of the pot. Try to keep these strips evenly spaced.

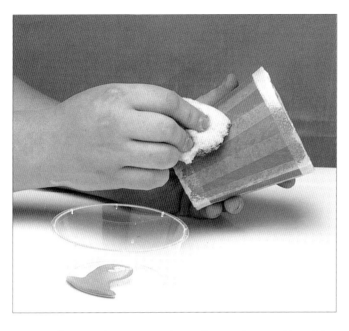

3   Sponge the opaque glaze all over the outside of the pot. Apply over masking tape to ensure complete coverage.

4   Allow to dry for a couple of minutes, then carefully remove the masking tape.

5   Paint patterns between the glazed areas using the 'free-hand' technique. The pot is now ready for glaze firing.

mexican hand-painted tiles

This project shows you how to decorate biscuit tiles with maiolica color. It is an inexpensive way to color glaze, as the color is produced from underglazes which can be bought in small quantities.

glaze

you will need

- ☐ Biscuit tiles
- ☐ Banding wheel
- ☐ Wide brush
- ☐ Lining brush
- ☐ Paper towels
- ☐ Tin-white opaque glaze
- ☐ Underglaze colors – yellow, red, blue and black

(You may want to add a few drops of a clear glaze to the underglaze colors to help them melt into the glaze)

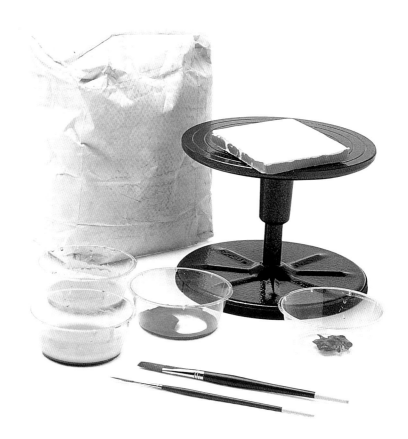

1 Hold the tile gently by the edges and dip it face down into the opaque tin glaze. Be careful not to splash.

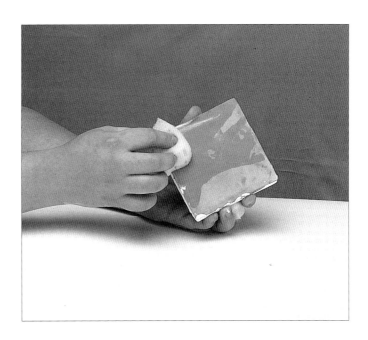

2 Clean any excess glaze from the bottom of the tile with paper towels.

3   Using the wide brush, paint half the tile with red underglaze..

4   Paint the other half with the yellow underglaze. Make sure the colors meet but do not bleed.

5   Center the tile on the banding wheel. Make sure the tile is well-centered to ensure an even banding.

6   Turn the wheel and band two blue rings onto the tile. Keep the wheel turning steadily to ensure an even color distribution.

7 Using a lining brush, outline the bands of blue with a black underglaze while spinning the banding wheel.

8 Paint a cross in the center of each tile using the black underglaze.

9 Then by 'free-hand', paint the line detail as shown. The tiles are now ready to be fired.

wax resist plate

This project is based on Indian Batik cloth design. As rougher lines produce a more effective finish, this is an ideal project for those with less than steady hands. This process is unsuitable for objects intended to have contact with food.

glaze

you will need

- ☐ Wax resist emulsion
- ☐ Fine brushes
- ☐ Orange and yellow glazes
- ☐ Sponge
- ☐ Scribe or knife

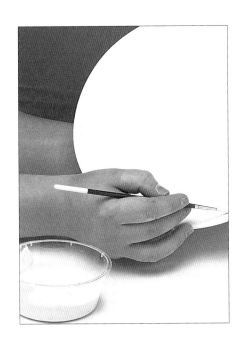

1   With the wax emulsion, free-hand paint a line around the edge of the plate. See template shown on p132.

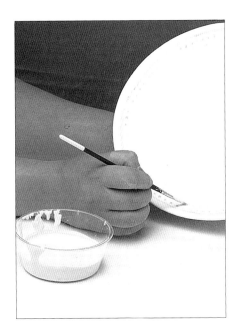

2   Paint dots of wax resist around the edge of the plate just under the first line, and enclose this with a second line parallel to the first.

3   Inside this line, paint small spirals of wax resist. Keep your pattern simple.

4 Now paint you central design. You may feel that your free-hand design looks rather crude at this stage. However, do not worry about this, as it will add to the batik effect. To produce the cracked batik appearance, take a scribe or knife and randomly scratch through the wax resist to the clay underneath.

5 Sponge the two colored glazes over the whole plate.

6 Apply two or three coats. This is normal for most brush/sponge onglazes. The plate is now ready for glaze firing.

blue delft

Delft pottery is a form of maiolica. This project shows
you how to make easy Blue and White china. Try not to
overwork the painted cobalt as the unfinished base glaze
may come off. Practice first on some scrap biscuit before
committing to a final piece.

you will need

- ☐ Biscuit fired jug
- ☐ Container
- ☐ Opaque tin-white glaze
- ☐ 1% cobalt carbonate in a water solution
- ☐ Fine paintbrush

1 Dip the whole jug into the tin-white glaze for a few seconds, then remove. Allow the glaze to drain off.

2 Mix up a solution of cobalt carbonate and water. An ideal mix is 1/25 oz (1g) of cobalt to 3fl oz (100g) of water. You should use no more than 3% as this will make the blue turn black.

3 Carefully paint a thin line of this solution around the rim and bottom of the jug. The lines will look watery, as the full color will not appear until fired.

4 Now paint random circles onto the side of the jug. Try to keep these evenly spaced but do not worry if pattern is not exact.

5 Starting just above one of these circles, paint a line vertically down to the circle. Stop just before you reach the circle. Outline this circle, then continue this vertical line down to the line around the bottom of the jug.

6 Repeat this process until the whole of the jug is covered with wavy lines. The jug is now ready to be fired.

The delft process can be applied equally successfully on flat surfaces. A template for this alternative project is shown on p133.

wax resist stoneware

This project will show you how to apply a varied thickness using a brush-on glaze. Alternatively you can try this method using two or three different glazes on one piece of ceramic. You can dip these layers rather than brush them on. (See Project 1, Two Tone Bowl).

glaze

you will need

- ☐ Paint
- ☐ Wide brush
- ☐ Toothbrush or stiff brush
- ☐ Brush-on stoneware glaze, variable with thickness
- ☐ Wax resist
- ☐ Biscuit fired bowl

1   Brush the first coat of glaze all over the inside and outside of the bowl. Do not overload brush and ensure an even coating.

2   Paint wax resist onto the rim of the bowl. Try to keep this band even and smooth.

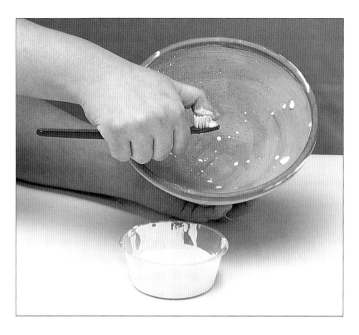

3   Dip the toothbrush into the wax resist and flick wax resist over the inside of the bowl.

4   Repeat step three for the outside of the bowl. Do this gently to avoid splashing yourself and your work surface.

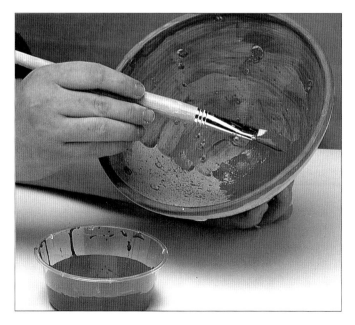

5   Once the wax resist has dried, paint another layer of glaze over the entire pot.

6   Once the bowl has dried, repeat the preceding two steps at least one more time.

7 You should build up layers until you have reached the required thickness of glaze. The bowl is now ready to be fired.

modern bowl

This project will show you how to slip trail a pattern onto an unfired glazed surface. It is advisable to test the combination first. If the ceramic is to be used as tableware, make sure the glaze combination is safe. (See Health and Safety, Metal Release, p16).

glaze

you will need

- ☐ Biscuit bowl
- ☐ Two brush-on stoneware glazes of contrasting color blue, oatmeal
- ☐ Slip trailer

Glaze the whole vessel with stoneware glaze.

2   Apply two or three coats altogether.

3   Mix up a thick glaze of contrasting color, and put it in a slip trailer.

4   Make sure slip trailer is securely fastened.

5 Pipe leaf detail inside the pot. See template shown on p134. The decorated piece can now be glaze fired.

onglaze

Paul J. Katrich. Pink luster vase.

Introduction

Onglazes consist of enamels and lusters that are applied to the surface of a fired glaze. They are very useful to the potter who has no interest in making but enjoys decorating, as you can buy the pottery you want to decorate. When applying enamels and lusters you should work in a very clean environment with new brushes. Try and get into the habit of having separate brushes for painting enamels and lusters. Any grease residue on the surface of the glaze will stop them from sticking. This includes dust and finger prints. If the surface needs to be cleaned it is advisable to wipe it down with a spirit based cleaner. (Use lighter fluid as a cheaper alternative.)

It is important when using lusters and enamels to think about the type of use the pot is going to receive. This is because the color or metal literally sits on the surface of the glaze and will wear off with excessive use. For tableware do not apply enamels to the center of a dinner plate as knives and forks will wear them away. Avoid putting metal/lusters on the edge of a mug or cup. Lusters and enamels will also wear off if you clean them in a dishwasher or use abrasive cleaning detergents.

Please pay attention to health and safety when using enamels and lusters. (See Health and Safety section, 'Fumes and Ventilation', and 'Metal Release')

The tendency is to buy only white-wear to decorate. A more dramatic effect can often be achieved by using a contrasting background color. This is particularly true of luster and metal effects. A good example of this is the use of blue and gold, popularised by the Sevres pottery in the 17th and 19th century.

The beauty of enamels is that you can re-fire the ceramic as many times as you wish, gradually building up the design. This is particularly useful when painting detailed work such as landscapes and townscapes. The translucent quality of the medium can then be truly exploited.

Paul J. Katrich.
Assorted lustered vessels.

How to luster an entire pot

1) Center the pot in the middle of a banding wheel.

2) Thin the luster if necessary with luster essence medium, or use cellulose as a cheap alternative.

3) Spin the wheel and gently apply the luster using a wide chisel brush.

4) Move the brush loaded with luster down the spinning pot. You will probably have to re-load your brush several times.

5) When you have reached approximately half way down the pot repeat the process from the bottom up to the middle.

6) Repeat on the inside of the pot if required.

You can buy lusters in a spray but these are more expensive and waste more.

Work in a well-ventilated area, especially when spraying lusters.

Judy Trim. 'Barcelona Moon', lustered bowl.

Jill Hunt Kitamura. Teapot. Maiolica glazed, stained red earthenware.

Gilding the edge of a plate

1) Center the plate on a banding wheel.

2) Load a fine detail brush with luster and place at right angles to the edge of the plate.

3) Gently turn the banding wheel leaving the brush static. You may have to reload the brush several times until the entire edge has been gilded.

Banding

1) When you want to band a metallic line on the inside edge of a plate you need to center the plate on the banding wheel as before and start it spinning.

2) Load a lining brush with luster and gently lower the brush, making contact with the surface of the plate. This is where you will need a steady hand

3) Allow the plate to make several revolutions before lifting off the brush.

Judy Trim. 'Green Storm', lustered bowl.

china mug

The first onglaze project introduces you to enamel decoration. Once painted, enamels will not take any handling, so masking off the panels to be decorated will reduce the amount of cleaning up you will need to do.

you will need

- [ ] White china or earthenware mug
- [ ] Enamel onglaze paints 4 colors
- [ ] Toothpick
- [ ] Masking tape
- [ ] Fine brush
- [ ] Wide brush

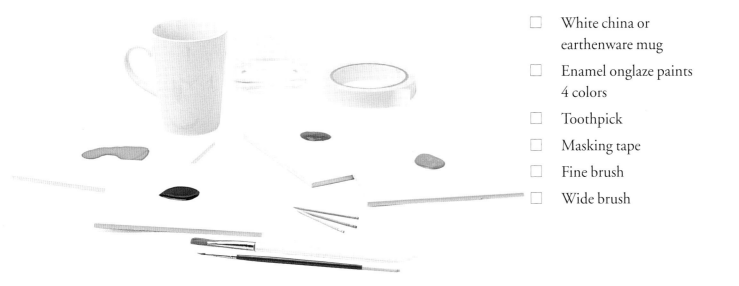

1 Mask off the rim and bottom of the mug using tape. Make sure the tape is placed evenly.

2 Using the handle as a guide, divide the mug into two panels. These panels should be of equal size.

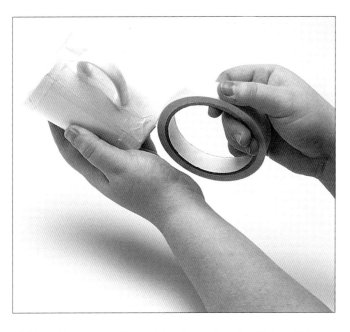

3   Also tape either side of the handle. This will leave white space alongside the design for a crisper finish.

4   Roughly paint over one of the panels. Use the wide brush to apply color in even bands.

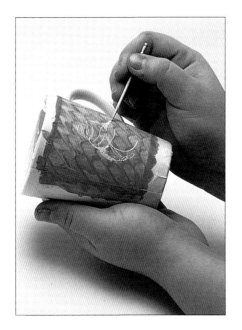

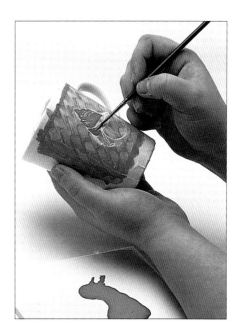

5   Before it dries, drag the wide brush over the paint with wavy horizontal lines.

6   Use a toothpick to etch the design onto the painted surface. Choose any design you wish. See template p136.

7   Now paint by free-hand the shell detail on top of the wave background, using the fine brush.

 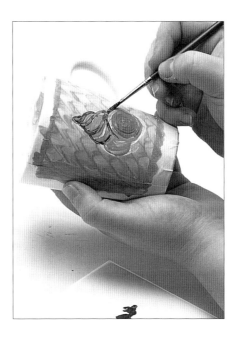 

8   Fill in the design using different colors.

9   Outline the pattern in a darker color. Leave this to dry.

10   Repeat the entire process on the other side of the mug. It is now ready to be fired.

You can use any pattern you wish to decorate your mug.

landscape plate

This project shows you how to achieve a basic
landscape. Once you have mastered creating a
landscape, try freehand painting detail such as buildings,
people, plants, or boats for a seascape.

you will need

- ☐ China or earthenware plate
- ☐ Enamel onglaze paints – blues and earth tones
- ☐ Tracing paper
- ☐ Sponge
- ☐ Paper towels

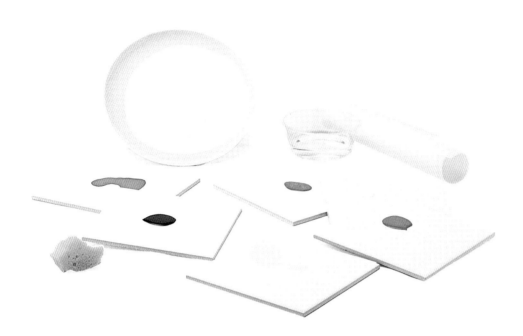

1 Over half the plate, sponge an enamel color to look like sky. You can mix different blue tones together to get a color you like.

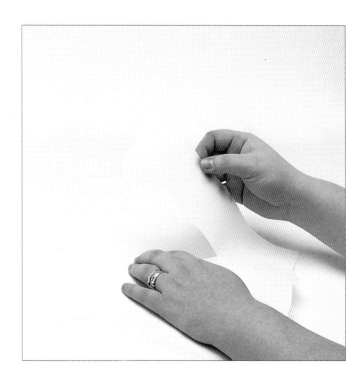

2 Tear some tracing paper into rough strips. These strips should be wide enough to lay across the plate.

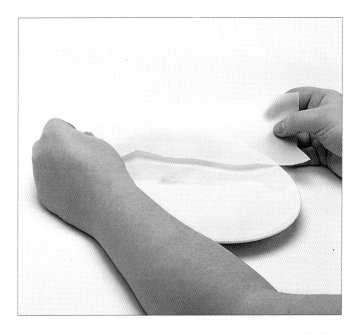

3 Making sure that the color you have already applied to the plate has dried, gently lay one strip on the plate, covering most of the blue, but allowing some overlap. This will form your horizon.

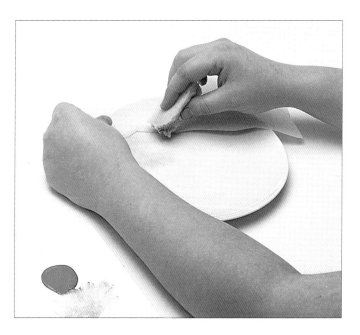

4 Now sponge an earth color up and over this paper mask. Apply the color as evenly as possible.

5 Once the enamel of this layer is dried, add the next strip of paper and repeat the process, using different colors, again until the entire plate is covered.

6 Clean off the edge of the plate with a paper towel. The plate is now ready for firing.

poppy jug

This project shows how to paint flowers onto a glazed jug. Liquid mask will allow the transparency of the enamel to show through without losing the crispness of the petal edges. The brush strokes will show, emulating the petal veins.

onglaze

you will need

- White glazed jug
- Liquid masking fluid
- Enamel onglaze paint – red, dark orange, black, green
- Fine brush
- Detail brush
- Toothpick

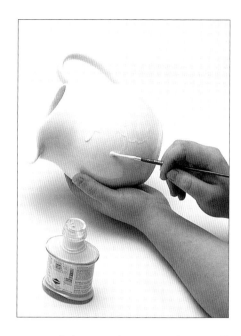

1 Paint rough poppy shapes all over the jug with the liquid masking fluid.

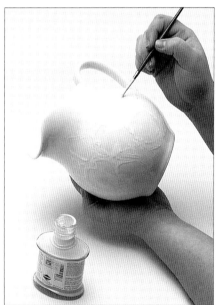

2 Fill the spaces between the shapes as much as possible with masking fluid.

3 Let the liquid masking fluid dry completely before continuing. Using a combination of a red and dark orange paint, fill in the unmasked areas with dragged brush strokes.

4 Work from the center of the flower shapes. This will help to create the petal veining.

5   When this has been completed, make sure paint is well dried before removing the liquid mask.

6   Carefully free-hand paint the black centers of the poppies using the fine brush.

7   Use a toothpick to scratch the black centers of each poppy so they are not completely solid.

8   Add the detail of the stalk in green. The jug is now ready to be fired.

mosaic bowl

Hand-painting a mosaic on a bowl can be a tedious
process. Using this method, however, is quick and easy.
When sponging the colors at the end, make sure the
enamel is not too wet, as the liquid mask may move.

- ☐ White bowl
- ☐ Banding wheel
- ☐ Earth tone enamels
- ☐ Liquid mask
- ☐ Detail brush
- ☐ Sponge

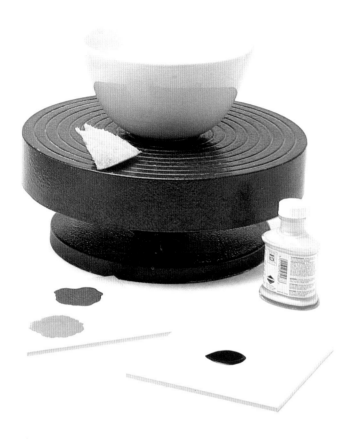

1 Place the bowl upside-down onto the banding wheel. Make sure bowl is well centered.

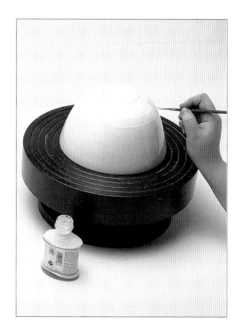

2 Now band a line of masking fluid around its base, using the detail brush. Repeat this at evenly spaced intervals down the side of the bowl.

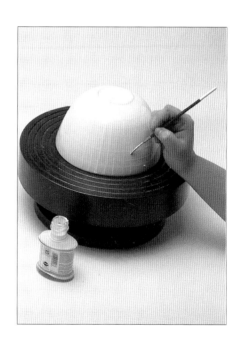

3 Now place the bowl onto the guide and paint lines of masking fluid vertically down its sides.

4   To create the mosaic pattern, paint a wave pattern over the already applied masking fluid.

5   Let the masking fluid completely dry before sponging earth colors over the entire bowl surface.

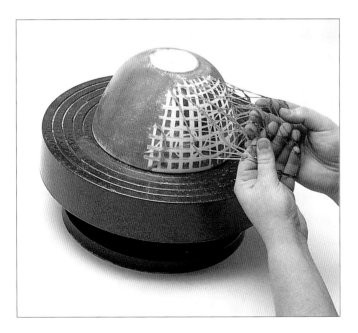

6   Remove the masking fluid when the enamel has dried. This will leave a clearly defined pattern.

7   The bowl is now ready to fire.

aboriginal design vase

For thousands of years, Native Australians have applied color using sticks. This project introduces you to decorating using tools other than brushes. Although this process takes considerable time and patience, the results are well worth it.

onglaze

you will need

- ☐ White-glazed cylindrical vase
- ☐ Tooth picks
- ☐ Wide brush
- ☐ Fine brush
- ☐ Onglazes – yellow ochre, brown

1   Paint a wash of the yellow ochre onglaze over the entire vase. Allow to dry.

2   Paint two brown stripes around the top and bottom of the vase with the fine brush.

3   Using a tooth pick, scratch diagonal lines down the vase from one brown band to the other. This gives you a series of panels.

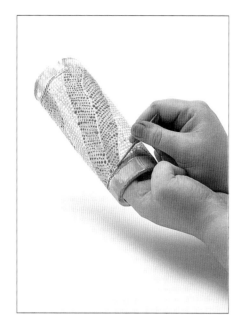

4   Using a broken tooth pick, now paint rows of dots in these panels. This technique is called 'pointillism'. Repeat this technique using alternative colors in each panel until the entire vase is covered.

5   When everything has dried, scratch through the brown bands at the top and bottom of the vase. It is now ready for firing.

Pointillism is effective on any shape or object. Template for alternative project – square vase – is shown on p135.

tiled table top

The easy availability of white-glazed tiles provides many
opportunities for the amateur potter. Decorated tiles can
be used for table tops, mirror surrounds and walls. This
project shows you how to stencil and overlay shapes,
allowing the translucency of the enamel to show
through to good effect.

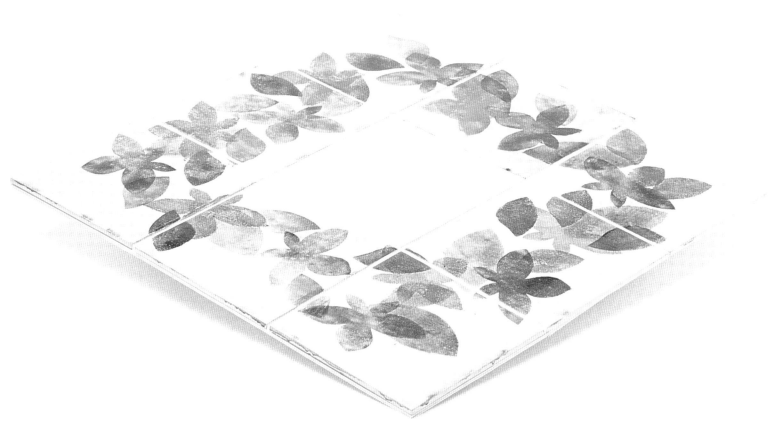

you will need

- ☐ 9 white glazed tiles
- ☐ Plastic for stenciling
- ☐ Craft knife
- ☐ Wide brush
- ☐ Sponge
- ☐ Light blue onglaze enamel
- ☐ Contrasting color onglazes brown, green, ochre

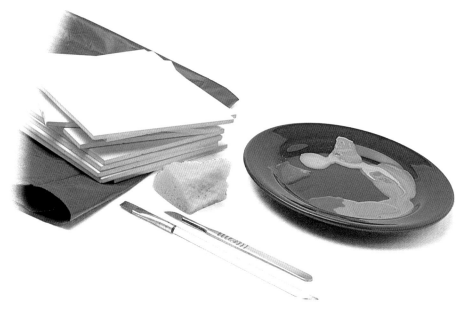

1 On a flat surface, arrange the nine tiles into a square.

2 Remove the central tile and brush the remainder with the light blue onglaze.

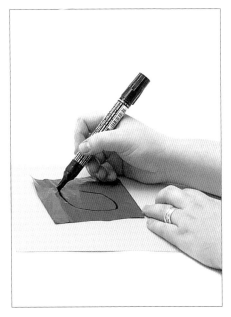

3 Using the stencil plastic, draw three leaf shapes. These can be the same leaf in different sizes, or three different shaped leaves.

4 Cut out the leaf shapes to make your stencils. Make sure you have spare plastic if you make a mistake.

5   When the background color has completely dried, lay a stencil onto the tiles, and sponge over the stencil. The stenciled pattern can overlap tiles.

6   Repeat this process until the whole border is covered.

7   Overlay a different stencil and, using a new color, repeat the process twice more.

8   The tiles are now ready for firing, and clear glazing if required.

stamped lustered plate

Luster is traditionally brushed or painted freehand onto a glaze. Making your own stamps is a way of controlling how the luster is applied. Always carefully read Health and Safety Guidelines (See Health and Safety, Fumes and Ventilation).

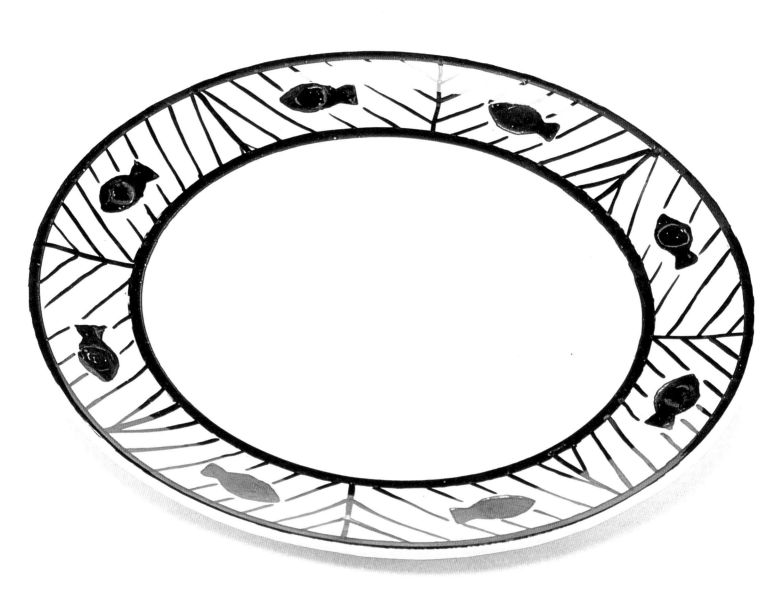

onglaze

you will need

- ☐ China or earthenware plate
- ☐ Copper luster
- ☐ Lining brush
- ☐ Liquid masking fluid
- ☐ Banding wheel
- ☐ Craft knife
- ☐ Wooden rod/stick
- ☐ Strong glue

1 Pour some liquid masking fluid onto a plate.

2 Leave this to set overnight until set hard.

3 When it has set, cut out a fish-shaped stamp using a craft knife.

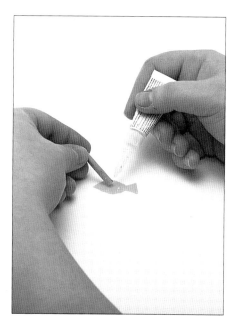

4 Stick this fish shape to the end of a rod or stick with strong glue.

5 Place the plate on a banding wheel. Make sure the plate is well-centered on the wheel.

6 Spin the wheel and band two bands about 1in (2.5cm) apart on the rim.

7 Dip the stamp in some luster and stamp it between the bands on the plate. Repeat this step around the plate until there are eight fish.

8 Between each fish, free-hand paint a line. This line should join the outer band to the inner.

9 Fill in these areas with diagonal lines. Try to keep these lines even. The plate is now ready for firing.

This technique can be applied to white or colored plates and any shape can be used

firing your work

Firing is one of the most important processes and you need to get right. Many pottery suppliers provide a firing service so if you are not attending a course in ceramics or do not own a kiln you can still make pottery.

If you over-fire your ceramic (exceed the maturing temperature), the color can burn out or the glaze can melt off. If you under-fire the ceramic the glaze cannot mature or turn into a glass, leaving the glaze or enamel matte. The order in which you fire your ceramic is also important. Apart from the initial biscuit firing the following firings must be done in descending temperature. For example glaze (high temperature), followed by enamels, and finally lusters. On all commercial glazes enamels and lusters you will find their maturing temperatures clearly labeled.

Preparing your work for firing

All work in a biscuit firing or first firing should be well-dried. For large items this can sometimes take weeks. Try and get into the habit of doing this slowly as fast drying can cause clay to crack. All items to be fired should have glaze-free footrings. If there is glaze in contact with the kiln shelf you will find your work welded there at the end of firing. You can wipe off the excess glaze with a damp sponge or use stilts to elevate your work off the kiln shelf.

You can hire kilns from local suppliers or colleges, or small electric kilns are a convenient size to buy.

The kiln

When you fire clay it turns into ceramic. To enable this you must heat the clay to high temperatures using a kiln. There are basically two types of kiln, a gas kiln and an electric kiln. The difference is that you can do reduction firings in a gas kiln and not in an electric kiln. There are two types of atmosphere you can have in a kiln, a reducing atmosphere and an oxidising atmosphere.

In a reducing atmosphere there is not enough oxygen available to complete the combustion process. To complete burning it cannot get more oxygen from the atmosphere so it gets it from the metal oxides in the clay

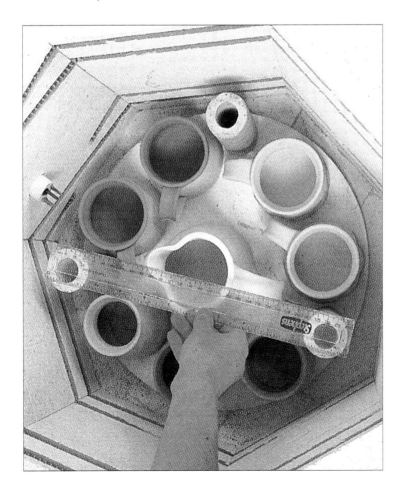

Always ensure that sufficient space is left around each object to be fired.

and glazes. This just leaves pure metal so the colors on the glazes will be drastically different. A reducing atmosphere usually produces more random and variable glaze effects. Many of the interesting glaze effects that a gas or reducing kiln atmosphere can make, can now be synthesised in an electric kiln.

In an oxidising atmosphere there is plenty of oxygen so the burning process does not have to rob oxygen from the metal oxides, in fact it actually produces an excess of metal oxides. The appearance of an oxidising atmosphere is clean, with no residual unburned fuel. It is therefore an important consideration when glazing your work not to apply a reducing glaze if you don't have a gas kiln.

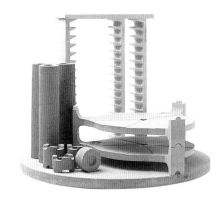

Kiln furniture, such as stilts, shelves and props help you to place objects efficiently.

Packing a kiln

There is a real art to packing a good kiln. To maximise the amount of items in a kiln you must take time to ensure glazed works are not touching one another. You can layer your work in the kiln by using kiln furniture. This is made from ceramic that can withstand temperatures in excess of 1300°C and comes in the form of shelves and props. Use three props when adding another shelf. Try and position shelf props above each other when stacking the kiln. This adds stability to the kiln furniture.

It is not advisable to mix biscuit firings and gloss (glaze) firings. This is because if there is any moisture left in the clay it has a habit of exploding because the moisture retained will turn into steam, and steam by its nature will have to try and escape. The violence of this action is illustrated well by looking at a boiling kettle. That is what happens when you don't dry your work out properly – the clay literally boils. If it explodes next to a glazed piece you will have bits of broken pottery welded to it.

Place heavier objects on the lowest shelf settings.

Temperature control

There are two ways of controlling the temperature in a kiln – manually or electronically.
When you manually control the kiln temperature, you use cones and minibars that are made out of refractor mixtures. Refractor mixtures melt at different graded temperatures. The way of telling your kiln has reached temperature is by looking at a cone you have placed in view of a spy hole. When the cone starts to bend the kiln has reached temperature. This is when you manually switch off the kiln. It is a good idea to use two cones when firing a kiln. One just below the ideal temperature and one at the ideal temperature. This forewarns you as to when the kiln temperature is about to mature.

Minibars melt in the same way as cones but are instead placed under or on a switching system inside the kiln. This means when the kiln reaches the maturing temperature the bar melts and physically switches off the power.

Electric controllers are an easier way of producing consistent results. They utilise an internal thermocouple that is attached to a pyrometer that senses the internal temperature of the kiln. This is connected to the controller and will turn off the kiln automatically when it has reached the required temperature.

Firing your kiln

Different stages in the making process require different types of firing. The first type of firing you will have to do on the way to a finished piece of ceramic is the biscuit firing.

BISCUIT FIRING

Due to the increased risk of the work exploding in this first firing, the temperature of the kiln must increase in slow increments. On a manual kiln there is an energy regulator that can be set at different percentages. It controls the amount of power being used by the kiln. This enables you to take the temperature up slowly. For example if you set the kiln at 33% it will take approximately three hours to reach the first temperature stage. If you set it at 100% it would only take an hour. The danger area for biscuit firing is in the initial stages. Water will smoke out of the clay up until around 120ºC. Chemically bound water to the clay molecules finish being released at around 350ºC. It is important that you ventilate the kiln well by removing any bungs and opening vents at this stage, to allow the steam to escape. It is advisable you to set the energy regulator at around 30% to begin with. Once it has reached around 400ºC in temperature, you can increase the energy output to around 80%. Replace the bungs and close the vents at this stage. Once it has reached 800ºC the ceramic is now stable enough to raise it up to 100 % or more.

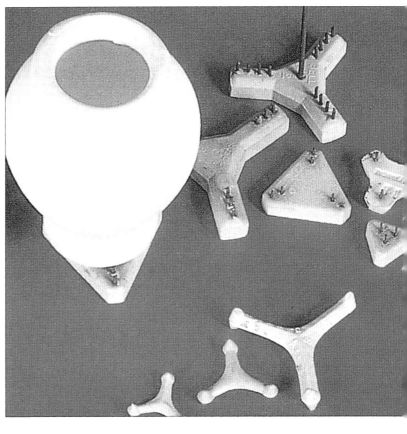

Small clay 'sitters' prevent fluid glazes from ruining kiln shelves.

Cones can be used to regulate kiln temperature. Once the cone starts to bend, the kiln is at the correct temperature.

GLAZE FIRING

The temperature of a glaze firing depends on the type of glaze. These can be of a low, mid, or high temperature. Glazes commonly start to mature at around 950°C. Potters commonly refer to these low temperature glazes as earthenware. Stoneware glazes have a firing range between 1240°C and 1260°C. Porcelain glazes mature between 1260°C and 1300°C. You will not need to exceed these temperatures.

The care needed for biscuit firing does not have to be repeated for a glaze. The ceramic has already had the water chemically removed from its body so there is no risk of explosion.

Some glazes will require a process called soaking. Soaking is when you keep the heat at a particular level for a specified time.

GUIDELINE TEMPERATURES FOR GLAZE FAMILIES

Earthenware . . . . .990-1060°C
Mid temp earthenware . . . . .1000-1160°C
High temp earthenware . . . . .1120-1180°C
Stone ware . . . . .1200-1280°C
Porcelain glazes . . . . .1250-1300°C

ENAMELS FIRING

Earthenware . . . . .760-800°C
Bone china . . . . .760-840°C
Porcelain . . . . .780-840°C

LUSTERS FIRING

The lusters used in this book are best fired in a well-ventilated electric kiln. Lusters can produce noxious fumes and should be ventilated until at least 400°C. (See Health and Safety section).

Earthenware . . . . .680-720°C
Bone china . . . . .700-740°C
Porcelain . . . . .740-800°C

When biscuit firing, ensure object is completely dry, and kiln is at correct temperature to prevent explosions.

UNPACKING A KILN

After successfully firing your kiln it is now time to unpack. You must not open the kiln until it has gone down to at least 200°C. If you open the kiln too early the glaze will craze or crack. This is due to the thermal shock of the cold air rushing in. Allow the atmosphere in the kiln to gently acclimatise to its surroundings.

Be careful when removing the finished glazed ceramic. Wear stout leather gloves to protect your hands from sharp glazes and hot pots.

Most kilns have safety features that stop the firing if the door or lid is left open. To make sure the kiln is safe turn off the kiln at the power source.

templates

Many of the projects in this book use very simple designs and patterns that you will find easy to recreate. You also have the option of using your own design if you prefer. However, a selection of the projects incorporate more complex designs, and for these we have included a template for you to use.

The following pages contain templates for 11 of the featured projects. Use a photocopier to enlarge or reduce a design to the size you require and trace it onto your clay or pottery blank.

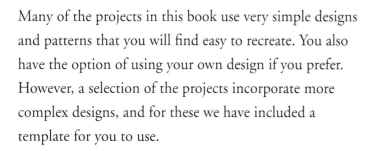

slip trailed panel

Pages 28-30.

relief model sun

Pages 34-37.

relief model moon

This template is for the complementary relief project shown on page 37.

intaglio pot
Pages 57-60.

combined techniques

Pages 61-64.

wax resist plate

Pages 83-85.

blue delft

This template is for the alternative project pattern shown on page 88.

modern bowl

Pages 93-96

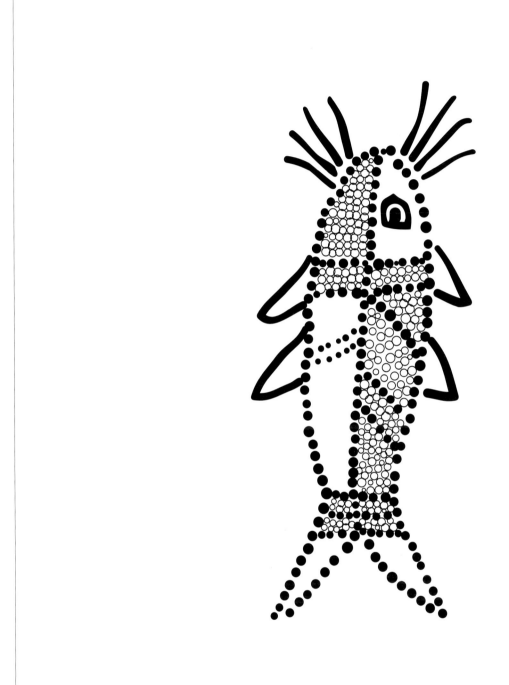

aboriginal design

This template is for the alternative project pattern shown on page 115.

china mug

Pages 100-103

sgraffito bowl

Pages 42-45.

gallery

There is a wide and diverse range of pottery decorating techniques in use today, with new methods still being discovered and created. The projects you have learnt in this book have provided you with a solid foundation of both practice and understanding which will be invaluable should you wish to go on to more advanced methods and designs.

The artists and ceramists featured in the following gallery section employ many of the techniques you have learned – or a variation – and we hope that you will be inspired by the beautiful and unique designs and effects they have achieved.

Caroline Fairbairn

Caroline Fairbairn is a ceramist, working mainly on commissioned models and specialist slip-castings. She also works with the National Trust on ceramic conservation.

Patterned vase.
Mother-of-pearl luster applied over white ceramic.

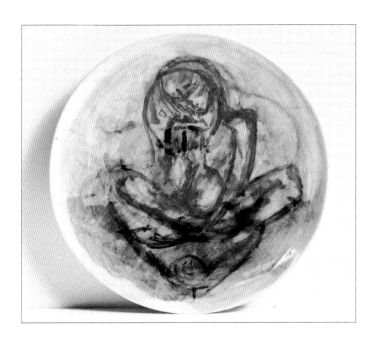

Figure plate.
Blue and mother-of-pearl luster applied over ceramic.

Banded vase.
Red color banded onto ceramic surface using banding wheel,
then clear glazed.

Arts & Crafts style plate.
Red underglaze with opalescent luster.

Spring teapot and mug.
Clear glazed.

Racing teapot.
Blue and white opaque glazes applied over a textured ceramic background.

Shaped vase.
Luster applied over a hand built and shaped vase.

Stephanie Allen

Stephanie Allen has been glass painting for several years and has been tutoring on glass decoration in London for two years. Stephanie also runs workshops and works on private commissions.

Painted tiles.
Vitrail glass paint and outliner paint over white ceramic. Mosaic tile painted using stencil, other three tiles free-hand painted using designs created by Liz Flaherty (oranges), Sally Ann Carver (lighthouse) and Lisa Hamdani (seahorse).

Dyana Symonds

Dyana employs a variety of onglaze techniques to decorate primarily bone china, but also porcelain glazed blanks. In general she mixes onglaze paints with an open medium, which means that the paint stays wet until fired. This allows changes to be made to the pattern before firing.

Plate with leaf pattern.
Onglaze paints on bone china, painted over a traced design. Kiln fired twice for depth of color, with initial firing at 780°C.

Fairy silhouette trinket box.
Onglaze paint mixed with black pen oil on porcelain, painted over a traced design. First firing at 780°C. Brush application of mother-of-pearl luster to the top. Carmine luster applied to sides first with brush, then sponged. Second firing at 760°C.

Art Deco Mug.
Onglaze paint mixed with black pen oil on bone china, painted over a traced design. Carmine luster applied to flower, with lilac luster on leaves. Fired at 760°C.

Mugs painted in Clarice Cliffe style. Onglaze paint on bone china. Crocuses painted freehand using a wide pointed brush for flowers, and a fine pointed brush for leaves. Initial firing at 780°C. Bands of color at top and bottom applied with a flat brush using a banding wheel, then fired again. Color mixed with dry medium to avoid dripping in the kiln.

Paul J. Katrich

Based in Michigan, Paul J Katrich specializes in hand-thrown vessels and bowls, fired with unique colors, glazes and treatments, including iridescent lusters.

Pink luster vase.
Variable pink lusters applied over ceramic.

Blue and green vase.
Ceramic fired after underglazing, then with alkaline glaze applied.

index

credits & acknowledgements

The author and publisher would like to thank the following for supplying much of the
materials and equipment used in photography.

Pottery Crafts
Stoke-on-Trent Head Office and South London Branch, UK

We would also like to thank the
contributors who allowed us to reproduce examples of their work:

Stephanie Allen
41 Bolton Road
Harrow, Middlesex
HA1 4SB

Janet Hamer
Lywyn-On
Coes-yn-y-Pant, Mamhilad
Pontypool NP4 8RE
Wales

Frank Hamer
Lywyn-On
Coes-yn-y-Pant, Mamhilad
Pontypool NP4 8RE
Wales

Paul J Katrich
Katrich Studios, Inc.
P.O. Box 1787, Dearborn
MI 48121-1787
USA

Jill Hunt Kitamura
22 Blackberry Trail
Concord, North Carolina 28027
USA

Silsal Ceramics
P.O. Box 1838
Amman
11118 Jordan

Mark Smith
11 School Lane
Sudbury, Ashbourne
Derby DE6 5HZ
UK

Dyana Symonds
12 Spareleazes Hill
Loughton, Essex IG10 1BT
UK

Judy Trim
3 Conningham Mews
London W12 9QW
UK